Living Blessed

THE MISSION STATEMENT OF THE BORN-AGAIN FOLLOWER OF CHRIST

LIVING BLESSED

THE MISSION STATEMENT OF THE BORN-AGAIN FOLLOWER OF CHRIST

Contributing author - Karen Martell
Editor - Don Jacobsen

Cover and interior design, Diane Baier

Cover photograph, Steve Cole Images, Atlanta, GA

Published by HighWalk Productions
PO Box 26, Hiawassee, GA 30546

ISBN 978-0-615-23972-9

Go to www.LivingBlessed.org for further information and also for other inspirational products by this author.

Contents

Dedication

Our friends, Forrest and Kathleen Preston, are sterling examples of living blessed.

He is a Christian businessman who loves the Lord and His people. Forrest has been a friend for more than 65 years and we have watched him and Kathleen exemplify the Christian grace of watching for people they can help, then extending their hands unselfishly.

They are respected and appreciated in their community and far beyond. It is a privilege for us to dedicate this book, *Living Blessed,* to them.

CHAPTER 1

Awesome Option

Voices of Lee
Lee University,
Cleveland, Tennessee

Danny Murray, director

After a magnificent gospel concert in Gatlinburg, Tennessee, my husband and I left the hall with the 10,000 or so others in attendance, still basking in the power of the music we had heard. Through Forrest Preston, a long-time mutual friend, we had been invited to have lunch with Danny Murray and the 16-member a capella ensemble from Lee University, called Voices of Lee, of which Danny is director. We joined them at a large restaurant near the hall.

The restaurant was filling rapidly when we arrived, but they found room to seat our whole group near one side. The place was electric as the customers ordered their food, and those who had been at the concert reflected on the inspiration they had just enjoyed. The noise level made conversation with anyone except the person next to you difficult. It was a joyous celebration.

As we finished eating and were preparing to leave, Danny nodded to the singers and there in the midst of that large restaurant, without announcement, they stood and began to sing.

The Lord bless you and keep you.
The Lord lift His countenance upon you,
And give you peace – and give you peace.
The Lord make His face to shine upon you,
and be gracious unto you,
The Lord be gracious, gracious, unto you.
Amen

The response in the restaurant can only be called amazing. The conversations halted mid-sentence. As the rich harmonies and the power of the words filled the place it became almost a sanctuary. No one ate. No one spoke. The servers stopped serving. The cooks peered through the kitchen doors. It was as if no one dared breathe. It was as though God Himself had made His presence known and that those same words He had spoken to Aaron in the desert centuries before He was now speaking to us. I doubt that many who ate lunch there that day left the same as they entered, since we are always blessed by the presence of God.

We tend to be, we believers, a bit casual with our use of the word bless. "Please bless mom and dad, and my sister Sally, and all my neighbors, Amen." Or, "… and bless all the missionaries and colporteurs in the foreign fields." Or something like this, "Oh, and bless this next litter of puppies so there will be enough money to pay Sam's tuition and he can stay in that Christian school."

Does He do that? Does God hear those kinds of drive-through prayers? Does the God who placed the universe and manages it have time to think about where I left my keys? To each of those queries the answer is a resounding, Absolutely. Of course. No question.

But God's understanding of a blessing is much bigger than that. It's as big as He is, because when God places His blessing on something or someone He gifts them with a part of Himself. Some of Him rubs off on them. He is no less, but they are much more. The majestic implications of that fact can cause you to lose sleep.

We read barely into the second chapter of the Scripture record before we see God selecting a day, a 24-hour period very like the other six —common, ordinary—and placing on it a part of Himself. It is now blessed, holy. It is now un-common; it is now extraordinary, it is now un-like the other six. It is unique, distinct, and carries eternal significance. His blessing changed a piece of time.

One of the Bible stories the kids love to hear is about Samson, arguably the strongest man we read of in Scripture. I mean, he caught 300 foxes (300 foxes, count 'em!), tied their tails together, set them on fire and burned up the crops and orchards of his enemies. So he was obviously pretty strong and pretty quick. Another time he was visiting a city on some illicit business and when he tried to leave in the middle of the night he discovered he had been locked in. No problem—he pulled up the huge gate posts, then hoisted the gates, the posts, and the beam that locked the gates onto his shoulders and carried them up a nearby hill. He destroyed a whole army legion with a weapon no more formidable than the lower jaw of a donkey. And even though Samson made some really bad choices you have to admit that he was a force to be reckoned with and he led his nation for twenty years.

Where did this daunting strength come from? We read nothing of any strength-training classes he took, no steroids, no gym membership or regular calisthenics program. But we do have this revealing statement about his early life: "The woman gave birth to a boy and named him Samson. He grew and the Lord blessed him. …" It is clear that we cannot separate *our* mission from *His* blessing.

Only a very few stories appear in all four

of the gospel accounts of the life of Jesus in the New Testament. Interestingly, one of those stories is about a miracle that occurs at a picnic. A major crowd has showed up on this grassy slope to hear Jesus preach, but when the sermon is over it begins to dawn on them that there are no restaurants within walking distance. So Jesus feeds them. In John's telling of the story he adds the interesting detail that Jesus took the lunch of a small boy, blessed it, then with it fed 5,000 families. It seems that even a sack lunch takes on a whole new role in God's plan when it receives His blessing.

Imagine then the awe of Living Blessed. Is that what the Apostle Paul meant when he described, "Christ in you, the hope of glory?" (Col. 1:27)

Living Blessed. Is that what the song writer meant when he wrote, "He touched me, and now I am no longer the same?"

Living Blessed. Is that what David was describing when he said a God-follower is like a tree that produces fruit and that "... whatever he does prospers?" (Ps. 1:3)

Living Blessed. Is that what He invites us to when He says, "You will receive power when the Holy Spirit comes upon you?" (Acts 1:8)

Living Blessed. He wants it to be more than a distant dream. He wants to create in us a strong Family likeness … His agenda and ours in perfect synch.

Living Blessed is not an event, it's a way of life. It's a miracle created by the touch of an eager God on the life of a willing disciple. Popular Christian author and educator, Andy Nash, says, "Rather than living a mostly secular life with some sacred around the edges, we should be living a mostly sacred life with the secular relegated to the edges." That's the stated purpose of the believer who chooses to live blessed.

Living Blessed is the mission statement of the born-again follower of Christ for whom walking with Jesus is not simply a recurring weekend event, but a passionate focus—or is it a focused passion? Both, I think.

If the history of Israel teaches us anything it is that God wants to heap His bounties on His children, but they often forfeit those gifts by choosing to live on the edges of His will. It isn't that He chooses to withhold His good things because we don't measure up to some arbitrary criteria. His gifts are not given to those who are good enough to deserve them but rather to those who have locked on to the cries of His heart and are committed to being useful for His purposes.

God has an agenda, you know. It is a breath-taking plan for the rescue of people He loves who were terrorized by an imported rebellion, then ravaged by participating in it. It broke His heart to think of spending eternity without them. "Jesus did not count heaven a place to be desired while we were lost." (Desire of Ages, 417) The more I ponder that thought the more unthinkable it becomes. Why would I ever want to live in a way that does not bring Him honor? In what could I ever find greater joy than to bring Him joy? Why would I ever make choices that did not permit me to walk in His story … by His side? Living blessed … in His presence … my heart His home … His plans, my plans … His will, my will. Awesome option.

That's our goal, isn't it, yours and mine. This chorus could be our prayer:

Lord, prepare me to be a sanctuary,
Pure and holy, tried and true.
With thanksgiving I'll be a living sanctuary
For You.

Living Blessed … the awesome option of being in-dwelt by the Absolute Sovereign of the universe who never met a problem He couldn't solve.

Chapter 2

A New Name

"I was a 'throw-away' baby," Philip reflected, tears coursing down his cheeks.

The seminar speaker, Pastor Jonathon Henderson, had just shared some amazing truths from Scripture about how God values His children and how He blesses us so we can bless one another—with *our* words and with *His* words. The speaker had talked about the exceptional power of the blessing God grants to each of us and how it changes us on the inside. It is God's intention—His joy—to lift, to encourage, to inspire. It's His nature to give and His glory to bless! And to us He gives the gift of being extensions of His hands.

Philip learned that all through Scripture—more than 200 times—the blessing is talked about. For Philip that day it was an amazing discovery. Apparently blessing His people is something God is passionate about.

He blessed Abraham, and told him, "I will bless you and you will be a blessing." (Gen. 12:2)

Jacob coveted the blessing—not the financial part of the birthright, but the spiritual. He even lied and cheated to get it, and his life was marred by those traits until he came to the Brook Jabbok. There as he wrestled with the Messenger from heaven he cried out, "I will not let You go unless You bless me."

God did bless Jacob. He changed his name to Israel, and He changed his character. Jacob then became a blesser. He blessed Pharaoh, the greatest reigning monarch on earth at that time—but Jacob was not intimidated for he had been blessed by the King of kings and Lord of lords.

Remember Esau's reaction to his brother's treachery? He wept and begged his father to bless him, too. Fathers blessed their children with words—showing their value. It was like a prophecy for their future, and both Esau and Jacob knew they wanted that.

It was God who directed the words of blessing that Aaron spoke there in the desert, precious words we still use today—we speak them and we sing them:

"The Lord bless you and keep you. The Lord make His face to shine upon you, and be gracious unto you; The Lord lift up His countenance upon you and give you peace." (Numbers 6:24-26)

But back to Philip, sitting alone near the back of the empty classroom. After the seminar, the room had emptied quickly as those attending rushed to their next appointments. Except Philip. He seemed riveted to his chair. The speaker was gone but as Karen Martell, the seminar hostess, was gathering up her papers she glanced back and saw him, sitting pensively, obviously moved by what he had just heard.

Philip was her friend, someone she prays for regularly. As she walked toward him she couldn't help wondering what had caused this strong emotion.

Philip looked down as he quietly described his past. "You don't know this part of my story, Karen, but I was a 'throw-away baby.' My mother was 14 when I was born," he recalled. "I never got to know her. She never wanted me. I was born at home, with only her mother present. They had a plan to dispose of me as soon as I was born. They put me into a plastic bag, and were getting ready to toss me into a dumpster outside their apartment. Providentially at that moment my great-grandmother arrived at the apartment. She grabbed me out of their hands, took me home with her and I became her special child. Growing up in her home was a huge blessing to me. She treated me as if I had value. She was a Christian, and she taught me about God. She helped me learn to forgive my mother and grandmother, and that lifted a great burden from my shoulders. She was a happy Christian and it was a joy to be part of her family.

"One day, when I was just a little guy, maybe 5 or 6, she came to me and explained that she had completed all the paperwork to legally adopt me, and now I would always belong to her. Then she said something that made me feel like I was someone of significance.

"'Now you have a very big decision to make.' she told me. 'You may choose any name you wish as your last name.' It's hard to explain just why, but, young as I was, that made me feel so important, so valued.

"When Pastor Henderson spoke today about the blessing, and how much everyone needs it, I realized, maybe in a new way, how really blessed I am. God sent my great-grandmother at just the right instant or I would not be here. It's really true, isn't it? God saved my life. I must have worth in His eyes.

"God told Jeremiah that 'before I formed you in the womb I knew you.' (Jer. 1:5) Even though that's true for all of us, somehow it had particular meaning for me. My great-grandmother —the only mother I ever knew—taught me that God is good. My home was a safe place and she has been a great blessing to me all my life.

"But the crowning act was giving me the privilege of choosing my last name, and for that I will always be grateful. Now I know that God loves me and has a plan and purpose for my life. I didn't want to choose my mother's name, and I never knew who my father was; I was so happy to take my great-grandmother's last name as mine."

Phillip gained new strength that day as he was able to see, in recounting his story to Karen, how faithful God had been in his life. His great-grandmother's loving touch, her prayers for him, were life-changing. He was truly blessed. Like Jacob, he had a new name, but more importantly, he knew who his Father was, and that he, Phillip, was part of a royal family. Living blessed … Philip knows.

For you and me, that's our story, too. When we were born, a determined enemy had already decided that he wanted our destruction. Eternally. He would shape every influence in his nefarious arsenal to keep us from God's best … temptations to entice us, companions to discourage us, circumstances to distract us, doubts to lead us off course, our own carnal natures to mislead us.

But at just the right moment a Rescuer appeared and snatched us from certain death, though the Rescuer Himself paid a price that would be conspicuous to everyone forever. Scars. Scars on His hands. Scars on His feet. Scars on his forehead. It's true, you know: When He was on the cross, we were on His mind. You. Me.

Unworthy—He made us worthy.

Undeserving—He took what we deserved so He could give us what He deserved.

Ponder it: Who are we that a King should die for us? But He did. He did.

How lavish His gifts: A new name—His. A wonderful family. A spot-free record in the books of heaven. A glorious, eternal future. We are not throw-away children; we are blood-bought. Redeemed. Rescued. "Snatched," as John Wesley would say, "from the burning."

No wonder God's people get up in the morning and before venturing very far into the day ask Him, "Who do You want me to bless for You today? Who do You want to love through me today? Who do you want me to put an arm around on Your behalf today?"

So with the new name He also gives us a new job: Blesser. Who's on your list today?

CHAPTER 3

The Grand Design

Someone once told me that the two most important days of a person's life are the day they are born, and the day they discover why.

In the grand design of the universe you and I are not intended to be receivers as much as we are to be channels, conduits, conveyors. Like any healthy body of water, we receive so we can give. All God has given you He gave for you to hand off to others. God instructed Abraham, "I will bless you and you will be a blessing." (Gen. 12:2)

Dr. Tony Campolo, professor at Eastern University in Philadelphia and a popular speaker and writer, had just arrived in Honolulu to speak for a large event there. On his first night in the tropics he was wide awake from jetlag and unable to sleep. After tossing in bed for a while he decided to go for a walk and get some fresh air; maybe a little exercise would help.

It was about 2:00 am, the weather was perfect—as it usually is in Honolulu—and he was enjoying the chance to stretch his legs after the long flight. A couple of blocks from his hotel he

spotted a little all-night diner and went inside.

Inside, everything he saw and smelled seemed to say, "Welcome to the original Greasy Spoon." The big man behind the counter—Big Al, the owner—wore not only a well-experienced apron, he also wore a big smile. "What can I get for you?" he asked.

Tony ordered a cup of coffee and a donut. As the rotund server reached into a large jar of donuts with his hand, he pulled out a not-so-fresh donut and laid it on a napkin in front of Dr. Campolo. It was, to say the least, a sad little offering.

As the server was pouring the coffee, the diner door burst open and in came half a dozen provocatively-dressed girls. They were loud and more than a little coarse. Tony quickly realized they were prostitutes from the street and must be on their "mid-shift break."

As he was thinking about how he could quietly slip out, he heard one of the girls say to the friend beside her, "Tomorrow is my birthday."

"So? What do you expect us to do about it, Agnes?" was the unfeeling response.

"I don't know," Agnes replied, "I have just been thinking about it, and wondering … I've never had a birthday cake."

This personal, very private comment fell on deaf ears—except for the quiet donut-eater from Philadelphia. It was dropped, completely ignored by her "friends" and the expression on Agnes' face couldn't hide her disappointment.

But the Holy Spirit was speaking to Tony, "Here is someone I love—someone I died for. She is valuable to Me," he seemed to hear God say. So when he saw the hurt in her eyes, Tony found himself silently praying for her. He asked the Lord to bless this girl, and to save her for His kingdom.

The girls didn't stay long and soon the little diner was quiet once again. "Did you hear what Agnes said?" Tony asked the café owner. "How can we give her a birthday party?" he asked wistfully.

"That's not a problem," was the answer. "Those girls are in here every morning like clockwork. They come in on their break, maybe get something hot to drink, and then go back out on the street."

"I'll bring the cake," Campolo offered. He was getting excited now. "Oh no you won't," the owner said. "That's what we do here. My wife is a great baker."

"Then I'll bring decorations and we can have a real party—tomorrow night at the same time," was Tony's enthusiastic response.

So the next morning, just before 2:00 am Tony and Big Al were hanging "HAPPY BIRTHDAY" banners, streamers, and balloons. Before long the little place was ready and looking for all the world like a good place to have a party.

At two o'clock sharp, as if on cue, the door burst open and the same group of girls noisily pushed their way inside. There was a large banner that said, "Happy Birthday Agnes" and a big round cake with candles aglow.

Tony and Big Al started the birthday song, and the girls joined in.

Happy birthday to you.
Happy birthday to you.
Happy birthday, dear Agnes,
Happy birthday to you.

Agnes was speechless. As she was regaining her composure Tony did something no one expected. He asked, "You know, since it's your birthday, Agnes, I'd like to pray a little prayer for you and ask God to bless you. Would that be OK?"

When the prayer ended, Agnes was struggling with her emotions; finally she looked at Dr. Campolo and the others and asked, "May I take the cake home?" Her eyes were pleading as earnestly as her words.

"I'll bring it back tomorrow, I promise, and you can all have a piece. I just want to take it home tonight."

"Of course, Agnes. It's yours," Tony replied. With that Agnes disappeared out the door with her precious cake in her hands. Even though that ended the party, everyone somehow understood that the event was huge for Agnes.

"I didn't know you were a pastor," Big Al observed after the girls had gone. "If I could find a pastor like you, I'd go to church every week." He sensed the genuine joy that the presence of the Holy Spirit had created there in his little diner that night.

Fast forward several years and Dr. Campolo is at a university in California where he is to speak for Commencement. As he reaches his seat on the platform, he sees balloons tied on his chair. "Who knew this is my birthday?" he wondered.

When he stood to speak, he found a small sign on the podium with these words: "Happy Birthday, Tony Campolo. With love, Agnes." There was also a card with a message that he will always treasure. Written on it was this note that took his breath away:

"I am sending this by a friend and I hope it

arrives at just the right time. I can't begin to tell you how the party in the diner and your prayer changed my life. I have a new life now. I work for Big Al right there at the diner. My life has joy, purpose, and meaning, and I just wanted you to know that."

God used a birthday party and a simple prayer to bless Agnes and change her life—forever.

That's God's Grand Design. The blessing prayer has great power because as we speak words of blessing we become an instrument of God's grace, an extension of His hands, a tangible way for Him to say to someone, "I love you." We are called by Him to do this. Notice:

"Finally, all of you … be tenderhearted, be courteous; not returning evil for evil … but on the contrary, blessing, knowing that you were called to do this. …" (1 Peter 3:8-9 NKJV)

God loves to bless His children because He can use them in turn to bless others. He blesses His blessers, and He distributes His gifts lavishly.

A blessing is redemptive and restorative because we become the vessels God uses to share His grace with others, often in unexpected places, maybe even like an all-night diner filled with ladies of the street. God moves us to see others from His perspective and then to love through us. Blessings are instruments of healing, and they very often have eternal consequences.

I'd like to encourage you to spend a few moments right now and reflect on ways that you can bless your family, your friends, colleagues at work, and relationships in your church and neighborhood.

That's what we watch for when we are Living Blessed.

Chapter 4

On Assignment

Karen Martell writes, "I pray every day that God will put people in my path that need Him and that He will use me as that instrument for change or encouragement in their lives. Opportunities often come at times and places I least expect them." A scripture instruction she loves to embrace is: "… be tenderhearted, be courteous, not returning evil for evil … but on the contrary blessing; know that you are called to do this. …" (1 Peter 3:8-9) Then it's an assignment.

"I learned a lot about that one day in the check-out line at Walmart," Karen recounts. "The lines stretched way back into the merchandise sections with busy Christmas shoppers and full carts, and few seemed to be in a very pleasant holiday mood. We chatted, read the magazines, and complained to each other, though none of those things seemed to help much in speeding up the check-out process.

"My turn finally came and I started to put my items on the belt when I sensed that my checker was not very happy. I couldn't get her to smile in spite of my attempt at some light-hearted banter. Ping … ping … ping … she was sliding the items through the scanner at a good pace when suddenly she picked up a bottle of bubble bath that didn't have a price on it. She let her exasperation be known.

"'What is the price of this item?' she wanted to know. 'I'm not sure,' I replied. 'It was on a shelf that said, '$2 - $5.'

"'Well, was it $2 or $5?' she pressed. I didn't want to say $2 if it was really $5, and I didn't want to say $5 if it was really $2; I honestly didn't know. She muttered something not very charitable under her breath and called for a floor clerk to come rescue her. By this point my agitation began to rise too, and I started mentally crafting all kinds of things I could say. I glanced at the line waiting impatiently behind me—longer now, if anything—and none of those folks looked very happy, either, about my bubble bath.

"Just as I was about to say something that wasn't remotely related to a blessing, God changed my mind. It was as though He spoke directly to me …' A faithful [person] will abound with blessing.' Those words meant that the blessing was in me to give away, abundantly, if I chose. I felt the stares of those behind me, but at that moment God melted my heart.

"The checker's face looked as if she were in the process of having a stroke and I don't think she expected to hear the words I said next; something like, 'This is a really busy day for you and I know I made it harder because I didn't know the price of that bubble bath. There is a very long line behind me, so let's just put it aside and I'll pick it up another time. It must be hard to keep your composure where there is so much pressure on you and everybody's in a hurry.'

"I told her I appreciated the job she was doing and that even though the line was long she treated every customer as if they were important. By now her countenance had completely changed. She was different. The corners of her mouth almost betrayed a faint smile. She was energized. I had blessed her with words that reflected God's perspective. Those words had encouraged her and totally changed the atmosphere at the head of the line. I left Walmart feeling that God had just made my day. He had blessed the checker, but perhaps, even more, He had blessed me."

Living Blessed—what an idea. Living under the giving hand of God. Living under heaven's agenda, not our own. Living on assignment. Huge ideas; all doable, not in my strength but in His.

My husband and I travel quite a bit and we very often find ourselves eating in restaurants. Recently we discovered a little plan that we believe honors God.

Sometimes, not always but sometimes, after we have ordered our food and the server is bringing it to our table, my husband will say quietly, "We are going to ask God to bless our food. Is there anything we can ask Him to bless for you?"

The responses have often been poignant. Sometimes we hear something very practical like, "You know, I have been having trouble with my wrist, and these trays of food are heavy. Would you ask God to heal my wrist?"

Recently one young lady replied, "When I'm here working my three young children are home alone. Please pray that they will be safe." Another said, "I have a family, I work full-time, and I am a full-time student. Please ask God to help me get everything done so I don't always feel like I'm running behind."

We feel honored to be allowed into the personal world of these folks and it is a privilege to pray for God's blessing on their lives. Sometimes they will tell us how we can pray for them, then turn and be on about their duties.

Other times they will stay at our table while we pray. Either way, God has blessed us so lavishly that we are privileged to pass that blessing on to others. We feel like this is part of Living Blessed, of being on assignment.

My friend, Kay, is receptionist for a major bank in our town. A former model, she's worked there for a long time and knows nearly everyone in our little town by name. We like to tell her that her very genuine smile lights up that whole part of the bank. A devout Christian, every day begins on her knees asking the Lord to send her people that day whom she can love for Him. Broken people, lonely people, hurting people, struggling people. And He does. In her special, unobtrusive, caring way seldom a day passes that she is not able to speak courage into the heart of someone who needs her gentle touch.

Late one morning I phoned her to ask a question and I noticed that there was a stronger-than-usual lilt in her voice. I said, "Kay, you sound especially happy this morning, what's happening in your world?" She answered, "Oh, Ruthie, God has allowed me to share His love with five people—and it's not even noon yet!"

Just today my husband and I stopped by Mountain Graphics, a printing company in our community run by Alec and Cyndi Therrel. They have become great friends; they do superb work and we share a deep faith in Christ. Cyndi seemed more effervescent than usual so we asked why.

Well, they had just returned from a cruise and they were still aglow. You have to understand that Alec and Cyndi make a living at the print shop, but their passion is to search for ways they can bless others. It's no coincidence that their daughter, Ashley, just returned from a six-month stint of mission service in India.

We asked about their cruise. "Well," Cyndi began, "we put into port at this little island off the coast of Honduras. We decided that rather than sightseeing or shopping we would try to find someone we could help." Aboard ship one of the crew had mentioned that there was an orphanage on the island that would welcome their visit, and maybe even be happy for some food for the children. Once ashore they found a taxi driver and explained their mission. "He blessed us," Cyndi recalled. "He was not only acquainted with the orphanage, he also knew the best places on island to purchase inexpensive food."

Cyndi continued, "I think the highlight of our whole trip was carrying that food up to the orphanage and seeing the joy on the faces of those little kids."

Living on assignment. Living Blessed. Living to be a blessing. Huge ideas; all doable—in His strength.

Karen again: "When we bless people—and things—we are dedicating them to God for His use and His purpose. In return He grants them His favor. This principle became a reality for me the day I walked into a local glass store looking for the perfect gift with a special etching on it for a pastor's wife. After some time, with the owner's help, I found a beautiful vase and gave him the words I wanted etched on the glass.

"It would read: 'You are to God the aroma of Christ, among those who are being saved and those who are perishing.' (2 Cor. 3:15)

"The owner loved the verse and confided to me that he was a Christian and was just struggling to keep his shop open even though he did all the work himself. When he finished our sale I made arrangements to pick up the vase the next day. As we talked about his shop for a few moments, I asked him if I could pray a blessing for him and for his business. He was thrilled. So I prayed a blessing on him and his business asking God to give him wisdom, talent for his work, to bless him with prosperity and multiply the fruitfulness of his hands. I also asked for the spiritual blessings that come from knowing and loving God and serving Jesus. I prayed that God would bless him with His promise of protection personally and in his business.

"The next day I went back to pick up my vase, and when he saw me he quickly came toward me, excited and talking fast. He told me that after I had left the day before, he went to lunch about one o'clock. He had put a sign in the window saying when he would return, then locked up the shop and went down the street to eat.

"An hour later when he came back, he discovered that his shop had been vandalized and robbed, the money had been taken from the cash register and valuable items had been stolen. They had left a mess of broken glass, locks, and a shattered window.

"I am standing there thinking, 'God, I prayed for this man and his business yesterday and I asked You to bless him with protection, and an hour later You allowed him to be robbed!' Frankly, I was stymied. Did God hear my prayer? If so, why didn't He answer it?

"What the man said rebuked me for my lack of faith. He continued: 'God protected me and

sent me out to eat. No one was in the store and I was grateful because I learned that the burglars had guns. If I had been here, I would have put up a fight and quite possibly would have been killed.'

"He continued, 'If you had not prayed for me I would not have left my shop. Thank you for blessing me. I am so glad that you prayed!'

"I paid for the vase, and as I left the shop, amazed by what had just happened, I thanked God that He had put in me the very words to pray for this shop owner as I blessed him with the promise of protection and safety. I thanked Him that I had been obedient to the promptings of the Holy Spirit and prayed on the spot with the owner.

"Does it make a difference when we pray God's blessing on people and things? Ask my shop-owner friend. He'll be happy to answer your question. I feel like I'm on assignment every day … an assignment with eternal consequences."

CHAPTER 5

Hope

Hope Stout

My dear friends,
I honestly can not
say how grateful I
am for you making a
donation to the Make-
a- Wish foundation.
Whether you gave a
dollar or 5,000 dollars,
Know that YOU made
a difference in some
childs life. And when I
see their wishes
coming true, MY wish
is coming true too!
All of this is because
you took a little time
to donate some money
and make a childs WISH
come true. I am sooo
grateful to all of you.
You did this. Thank you!
~Hope Stout~

I'd like you to meet Hope. Happy, funny, perky, pretty, 12-year-old redhead. Hope Elizabeth Stout was the youngest of three daughters, in 7th grade, a high energy, all-star member of her school's basketball team, cheerleader, tumbling enthusiast, high-speed inner-tuber behind the family boat. You get the picture—high energy.

One early-June morning in 2003, Hope's mom noticed that she was limping a bit as she walked. Yes, her right knee was bothering her, Hope admitted, but, they agreed, no doubt a pulled muscle or some other normal 12-year old's malady. When it didn't get better they scheduled a routine visit with their family pediatrician; that didn't help either. Probably "growing pains" he concluded, not serious enough to order an X-ray. After all, she'd grown four inches in the last year.

I am indebted to the book, *Hope's Wish,* written by Hope's dad and mother for many of the details in this story. I encourage you to read the full account.

Hope's discomfort increased and would finally create a pain level that was intolerable. On Friday, June 27, 2003, she was diagnosed with a rare form of bone cancer, osteosarcoma. Within a few weeks the tumor had invaded her upper leg, hip and back, and had metastasized to her shoulder and one lung. The Stout family—dad, mom, and all three daughters—were strong Christians and were convinced that God would heal "Little Red" (as the OB nurse had called her) miraculously so that her story could be told and it would bring God glory.

Yet, short of divine intervention the future began to look increasingly uncertain—or worse. Their trust in God was enormous, but they could not dismiss the thought that God might elect to answer their prayers in ways different than they would choose.

Difficult surgeries, weeks of chemo, and uncounted trips to the hospital later, the oncologist began to use the word "terminal." The tumor in Hope's right knee was growing at an aggressive rate, movement was becoming increasingly difficult for her, and pain management became a round-the-clock issue.

Enter Make-A-Wish®

The Make-A-Wish® Foundation is an organization whose sole purpose is to bring happiness to kids with life-threatening medical conditions. Every 38 minutes on average, since its inception in 1980, the Foundation has granted a wish to a youngster, totalling more than 155,000 kids to date.

Generally, on recommendation of the attending physician, Make-A-Wish® contacts the family and offers to provide funding to fulfill any wish the young person might have. It is truly a mission of mercy as it provides the child and their family a diversion—albeit temporary—from the reality they are facing.

The youngster may wish for a trip to Disney World. Or to meet a celebrity, or maybe a sports star or famous musician. They may ask to visit a theme park and swim with the dolphins, or maybe attend a Super Bowl. Some of the requests get pretty exotic ... Jose, a 4th grader, wished to have a new playground installed at his school. Ethan, a 10-year-old from Maine, wanted to go on a dinosaur dig in North Dakota—which he did.

Make-A-Wish® receives the request, takes it to their Board to make sure it falls within guidelines, then sets about raising the money

to fund it. In 2003 the average wish project cost about $5,500.

On November 19, two "wish granters" from Make-A-Wish® arrived at the Stout home to begin discussions about how they could grant the wish that might bring Hope and her family a memorable time of joy. After introductions one of the ladies said, "We are here to grant your wish, Hope; whatever you want." Now there's a blank check for a 12-year-old!

The Stouts were thrilled to learn that the students from Hope's older sister's high school had already raised nearly $8,000 to fund whatever wish Hope might make. But Hope surprised the four adults in the room with her next question: "So, other kids are getting wishes too … right?" "Yes," was the guarded reply, "we are working with lots of other kids. We get their requests and then we work to fund their wish."

Hope pressed, "Are any kids waiting on money for their wishes?" "Oh, yes, we always have a waiting list," the representative explained.

"How many kids are there who are waiting to have their wish granted?"

After comparing notes for a moment, one of the granters replied, "About 155 in our region."

"How much would it cost to grant every

one of those requests?"

The Q&A had just veered in a direction no one anticipated and it took a few minutes for the visitors to catch their breath, then come up with the answer. "Well, it costs about $5,500 on average, so that would be a total of more than $850,000."

"OK, that's my wish," Hope responded. "I want to grant the wish of all of the other 155 kids."

It felt as though all the air had been sucked out of the room. No one spoke. The two visitors looked at each other, at Hope, at her parents, then tried to suggest other options. Hope was not in the mood to negotiate. They had asked her for her wish; she had given it. But it would cost nearly a million dollars. It *was* a bit out of the norm.

Some small-talk later the visitors left, promising to take the request to their Board. Thus began an unprecedented project that was born in the heart of a 12-year-old.

Everyone knew that time would be a factor because of the rapid progress of Hope's disease. Donations began to come from everywhere … school kids emptied their piggy banks, a homeless man came to the project office and dropped a few coins into a container there. Corporations sent checks. Teens turned in their baby sitting earnings.

Churches passed the offering plates.

The week before Christmas, after Hope was interviewed on a local talk show, the people of Charlotte and the surrounding area opened their purses and their hearts to this plucky 12-year-old with a heart 155-kids wide. And no wonder. Here is some of what she said in that interview:

> "And just to, uh, just to see their smile and to know that I made a difference in their life is just an amazing feeling, and it's far better than any other wish, like to go to the Bahamas or something, or be famous. … It's just that feeling that you get that you know you made a difference in some kid's life. It's just amazing. …"

When asked by the host, Keith Larsen, if this didn't seem like too ambitious an undertaking, Hope matter-of-factly replied:

"We're just giving it to God, and He's gonna take care of it. Have a 100% faith in God, and anything is possible."

Later, Hope would say, "To be famous for being on a television show is okay, but to be famous for bringing people hope is even better." That would become the focus that energized everything she did, and galvanized a city—including its professional football team,

Kevin Donnalley, offensive guard, Carolina Panthers football team, with Hope Stout.

the Carolina Panthers, led by Kevin Donnalley, offensive guard and one of Hope's biggest fans.

On Christmas Eve 150 friends and supporters holding lighted candles gathered on the Stout's front lawn to sing Christmas carols and pray for Hope. Shelby, Hope's mom, stood on the front porch, stunned that so many would leave the warmth of their own firesides on Christmas Eve and show their love and support for a 12-year-old girl. Later she would observe, "It was the best gift we could receive this Christmas … This is exactly what Hope was teaching us with her wish: To think of others before thinking of ourselves."

At 8:35 pm, January 4, 2004, with her family around her, Hope Stout lost her battle with osteosarcoma.

Three weeks later, January 16, more than a thousand people attended the Celebration of Hope event in Charlotte to tally the donations that had been made to fulfill her wish. When the funds were counted, $1,116,000 had been received. As I am writing this, more than $3,000,000 has come in to grant the wishes of hundreds of kids throughout western North Carolina. David Williams, president and CEO of the Make-A-Wish® Foundation would say that night, "Hope, you did more to impact our world in twelve years than many of us will in a lifetime, and your legacy lives on."*

I have wept often as I have been absorbed in the story of Hope and her remarkable family—Stuart and Shelby, and Hope's two older sisters, Austin and Holly. It has led me to ask some important questions: What might the assignment, "living to be a blesser" look like? What can be the impact of one person—even a youngster—who decides to put others first? Also, what are the

---

*You can see an update of the project at http://marchforthwithhope.com/hopes-wish.

influences in the life of a young person that can help develop those qualities?

It's not an accident.

It has also been an ennobling experience for me to explore the story of the Stout family and to get personally acquainted with Stuart and Shelby. Here's a yard-marker I discovered in their journey: Shelby observes, "Stuart and I tried to teach our girls at a young age to help others in need whenever possible." And it was not just with lectures. The Stout's church—Matthews United Methodist, in Charlotte—conducts a "Rainbow Camp" each year for special-needs kids. For a week each summer kids with downs syndrome, autism, cystic fibrosis, and other life-complicating issues are taken to Rainbow Camp. Each camper is assigned a youth who has been trained for this special ministry who is their overseer. Each camper also has a "camper buddy," whose sole job is to be beside them as a friend. Hope began serving as a camper buddy each summer from the time she was seven.

When Hope was ten she was asked to make a list of her dreams for the future. In her list she wrote:

- Better handwriting
- To be a Marine Biologist

- To be President
- To make the world a better place

The first three we might predict—remember she was ten—but it's the fourth one that says so much about her character. The environment in the Stout home was building in her a heart to serve.

Each summer their church also sponsors a REACH work camp. They select a rural community somewhere in the southern part of the US, then raise their own funds and refurbish homes there. It is transformational to the communities where they work as well as to the folks who live there. Hope and her sisters worked right alongside Dad and Mom on these annual mission trips, down on their hands and knees nailing flooring or hanging from a ladder painting window frames.

The Stout family's deep faith in God was an anchor to their three daughters. Hope was an active member of the Core Club, a seven-member Bible study club for pre-teens in her community. It was here she developed a deep love for the Bible and a passion to pray. Not long before she died she wrote in her journal, "I know that when I don't have the strength to pray, you listen to my heart, Lord. I love you and I need you."

That kind of intimacy with God shapes

character. Late in the development of her disease, her mother was expressing her grief to Hope and told her how she wished she could take the suffering on herself. Hope replied, "Mom, I would never, ever let anyone take this journey for me, even as bad as it is."

During the radio interview on November 28, in response to a question posed by the host, Hope said, "My being different is good because since I have my cancer which has made me different, I can show others back to their faith and inspire others to be closer to God. I am very grateful to be different. I have changed people's lives." She was twelve.

David Williams, president of Make-A-Wish® was right: Hope's legacy indeed lives on. The same is true for all who choose, as Hope did, to honor God by living to bless.

CHAPTER 6

Living Forgiven

Dr. David Levy,
author, *Gray Matter*

Let me tell you about the man who tried to buy an unusual hat. Do you know the name Rogers Cadenhead? His story is a classic example of the need of the human heart to be forgiven. Sometimes the biggest blessing we can give someone is to forgive them—or to help them forgive someone else, or themselves.

Rogers Cadenhead lives in St. Augustine, Florida, and he buys and sells internet domains. In 2005, when Joseph Cardinal Ratzinger was chosen as Pope following the death of John Paul II, Cadenhead rushed to purchase the domain names for all of the papal titles he thought Ratzinger might ever choose—for $12 each. He suspected the new Pope might choose the name Benedict, so he bought, for instance, PopeBenedictXVI.it; PopeBenedictXVI.va; PopeBenedictXVI.com; PopeBenedictXVI.net; PopeBenedictXVI.org; and PopeBenedictXVI.info. He was right; Ratzinger chose Pope Benedict XVI as his title.

Not long after, Cadenhead was approached by officials from the church who indicated an interest in buying the domain names from him. It's a common practice, and "cyber-squatters" as they're called, will often hold celebrities or new companies hostage to get a large sale price.

Cadenhead made an interesting decision. As a former Roman Catholic there were some things that still bothered him about his past so he made the Vatican officials a rather irregular offer. He offered to donate all of the PopeBenedictXVI domains he owned to the Catholic Church at no cost, but with this caveat:

Rather than asking for money he asked for three favors. First, he asked for one of the "hats"—his word for the special tiara worn by the cardinals. (Incidentally, that request was denied). He next asked for a week at one of the luxury hotels at the Vatican. (I suspect that this request wasn't granted, either.) But his last request was the most unique: Cadenhead asked for total and complete absolution from all sins committed during the third week of March, 1987.

Remember that these negotiations were taking place in 2005; in 1987 Cadenhead was 19 or 20. Whatever had happened that week in March, no matter that he had often asked forgiveness, he still—18 years later—had the sense that in a record book somewhere the sins from March,

1987, were probably still being held against him. If only someone could have helped him grasp the reality of God's forgiveness—total, unearned, unequivocal.

It is not uncommon for us to find those who have difficulty receiving the blessing God wants to give them because they are unable to receive—or to extend—forgiveness. Listen to Dr. David Levy, author of the book, *Gray Matter,* as he describes the relationship he discovered—as a practicing neurosurgeon—between forgiveness and healing:

"When I first began praying for my patients, I had no idea that it would lead me to discover the power of forgiveness. The idea that bitterness was the source of health problems would not have made sense to me earlier in my career, but over time I became convinced that one of the greatest thieves of joy and health is the unwillingness to forgive the people who have hurt you."

This prominent surgeon, who has life-saving success with delicate surgeries for complicated procedures such as brain aneurysms, writes, "I had confronted this lesson in my own life. After years of being critical, judgmental, and even envious of people I blamed for my shortcomings and failures, I came to realize that bitterness and envy were affecting my health and my enjoyment of life. When I forgave these people, I felt empowered to truly live. I became freer and happier, less driven to perform, less anxious, less insecure. ... When I forgave my father but not stopping there—I ended my destructive cycle and began to change. It allowed me to see how to care for people in a new way, more selflessly than before."

Dr. Levy goes on to say that although he knew smoking was a deadly habit and often confronted his patients about it, he had the growing conviction that resentment and bitterness also caused some diseases and inhibited healing in others. He decided to bring the subject up with more of his patients to see what results he got, though he had no idea it would be so effective.

Levy tells about Ron, a patient who had a dangerous tangle of vessels in the dura mater, the covering of the brain. He had serious symptoms and his situation was potentially grave. After he and Ron discussed the symptoms and possible treatment plans, he said something the patient was not expecting. Dr. Levy recalls the dialogue:

"'Ron, there is something else I want to talk to you about,' I said, clearing my throat and calling forth my boldness. 'I want to make sure that you have every chance of healing from the surgery, and that means having good emotional health as well. Emotions can significantly affect the health of our bodies, for good or ill. Stress, anger, and resentment can have powerful negative effects on the body,' I told him. 'Bitterness is like an acid that eats its container.

"I looked this massive man in the eye. 'Is there anyone you have not been able to forgive?' I asked.

"He looked directly at me now, stunned. His eyes grew big and serious. An angry look passed over his face. He opened his lips, but no sound came out. …

"After a few long, painful seconds he deflated in his chair, dropped his head to his chest, and said something I didn't expect.

"'My mother.'

"This man, who looked every inch the fearless marine that he was, had just acknowledged being poisoned inwardly by bitterness toward his mother.

"'Do you want to tell me about it?'" I asked.

"Without hesitation he began to talk, describing a sad tale of abuse and abandonment by a number of different people. Ron had felt rejected when his mother chose to stay in an abusive relationship with a boyfriend who mistreated Ron.

"'I can understand your feelings,' I said. 'You have suffered injustice and you have every right to be angry. I do think that this is hurting your health and stealing much of the joy from your life. Bitterness is like poison that you swallow hoping that someone else dies. I am going to ask you to do something very courageous.'

"I paused for a few moments.

"'I think you need to forgive.' I said. 'I don't want to push if you're not ready to let it go, but if you're ready, I would be happy to help.'

"'Jesus made a very serious statement,' I told Ron. 'He said that if we forgive others their offenses, God will forgive us. If we don't forgive others their offenses against us, God will not forgive our offenses.'

"He looked genuinely surprised. 'I didn't know that,' he said.

"'I would like you to repeat a declaration of forgiveness. Think about what I'm saying, and if you agree, say it in your own words.'

"'Okay.'

"'I choose to forgive my mother for the things she did and didn't do that hurt me.

Specifically I forgive her for … now you continue. What do you want to forgive her for?'

"'I forgive her for making poor choices.' As soon as he spoke, he began to weep. 'I forgive her for thinking only of herself and not her kids,' he continued. It was as if he had been waiting to say this for years. 'I forgive her for drinking and not taking care of herself.' Ron went through a long list of specific things and as he did, he was weeping loudly.

"When he finally finished, I said, 'Now would you like to ask God to forgive you for holding these feelings of resentment and bitterness against your mother?'

"He was so ready, he didn't wait for my words, he offered his own.

"'Do you have other things you'd like to ask forgiveness for?' I asked. He nodded and asked for cleansing and forgiveness for his own personal list.

"'How can God forgive our sins?' I asked.

"'Jesus.' he said simply.

"We sat silently for a moment. I was still marveling at how the scene had played out.

"'Very courageous,' I said. 'How do you feel?'

"He dried his eyes and looked up with a big

smile on his face.

"'I feel like calling my mother,' he said. 'I can't wait to talk to her. Doc, I feel great, like a brand new man.'

"He hardly looked like the same individual who had walked in. His countenance had gone from stone to sunlight.

"Three weeks later I operated on Ron. It was a difficult but successful procedure. I saw him several times post-surgery, and he said his newfound joy was so strong that nothing could dampen it. His mother had recently turned her life around and had started attending church. The family was planning a reunion.

Dr. Levy reflects: "This was my first experience with offering to help a patient forgive, and I have never seen a drug or an operation with that kind of transforming power." Forgiveness had turned a tough, angry, ex-marine into the portrait of childlike joy.

Have you forgiven those in your life who have hurt you? Have you forgiven yourself? When you go to God for forgiveness, accept it, thank Him for it, and leave your burdens with your gentle, loving Friend.

Sometimes the biggest blessing we can give someone is to forgive them—or to help them forgive someone else, or themselves. Granting and accepting forgiveness are part of Living Blessed.

Incidentally, Dr. David Levy, quoted above, knows something about giving and receiving forgiveness, too. In the dedication of his book, *Gray Matter,* he wrote:

> "This book is dedicated to my father, Isaac Levy, who passed away in 2001.
>
> Dad, you were a man of integrity and hard work, on whose shoulders I now stand. You demonstrated courage in the face of adversity, and only now do I realize all that you gave me.
>
> After we reconciled in 1997, I asked you to give me a father's blessing. You wrote, 'That you may be happy in your work and in your endeavors … and that you continue growing.'
>
> This book is the fulfillment of that blessing. I know that we will meet again, and when we do, we will have much to celebrate."

Chapter 7

Blessing the Family

A strong custom that has survived through the centuries in many Jewish homes is the blessing of children. Jesus apparently was familiar with the practice because Mark records (Mark 10:16) that "… He took the children in his arms, put his hands on them and blessed them."

We know of a church in Savannah, Georgia, that places an ad in the newspaper early in the autumn and invites parents from the community to a special service where they pray a blessing on their youngsters who are about to begin a new school year. Scores of families who don't attend any other time during the year show up for this special service. I believe that a prayer of blessing for a child is a prayer Jesus loves to answer. You may or may not want to advertise in the press, but how about a special blessing of the teachers in your congregation. And a blessing for the students of all ages who are part of your church family. Let's not act as if they no longer need the blessing of God because they are in college!

A dear friend in Louisiana told me an interesting story. As a child she would pause every morning at the front door before leaving for school, and either her mother or her father would come and place a hand of blessing on her head and pray a short prayer for her, asking God to be with her, to protect her, and to give her His special blessing for that day.

What an enormous gift. She recalls how she came to expect special evidences of God's presence and protection because her parents had asked Him. Priceless heritage. The interesting part of the story is that she assumed every one of her classmates received the same send-off from home each morning. She was in her teens before she realized that it wasn't a common practice in every Christian family. What a strength it would be if it was.

My niece and her family were teaching in a Christian school in North Dakota, and in the spring they loved to visit my husband and me in Florida so they could "thaw out," as they put it. One Friday evening we invited them and their two children to join us on the back deck for a special blessing. Jordy was nine and when it came his turn we put him in the center of the circle.

Each of us told him how we saw God at

work in his heart and that we believed God had an important work for him to do. Then we placed our hands on his shoulders and in turn prayed that God would anoint him, empower him, and walk with him daily. It was a special moment for our entire family.

The next spring they came again, and as they were preparing to leave for home, Jordy, 10 now, came to me obviously with something on his heart. "Auntie Ruthie," he began, "we didn't play our game this year."

"What game is that?" I asked.

"You know," he replied, "the one where I was in the circle and everybody said nice things about me and then prayed that Jesus would help me be strong. I cried, but no one knew it … it was dark out there; but I was warm inside."

Time will probably never erase that memory from his heart whenever he recalls, "I was warm inside."

Lynn and Karen Martell decided to give a meaningful gift to their son, Todd, at his wedding reception. The event was held in the parents' home with nearly 100 family and friends there to share in the celebration.

After the meal the guests gathered around Todd and his bride, Axa, as Lynn and Karen blessed the new family. Placing hands on them and quoting frequently from Scripture, the parents sought God for His guidance on the decisions the new couple would make, that He would provide wisdom, keep them strong to do His will, that they would watch for opportunities to bless others, and that they would become all God intended them to be.

The guests were in tears when the blessing was completed; it was a memorable moment for all who where there. For Todd and Axa it made the significance of their wedding complete.

In scores of places across North America and in other countries as well, we have conducted a blessing service for the pastor and spouse of the host church, the conference president and spouse or other denominational leader, prayer ministries coordinator, or local church elder.

Some have asked that we write out the details of the service, both to serve as a validation for the service and to provide an outline of what we do and why, though there is no formal order of service.

The person or couple chosen come to the front of the church and sit facing the congregation. The individual leading out may spend a little time explaining the significance of the blessing. They

might tell of Jacob's wrestling with the angel at the Brook Jabbok when he would not surrender unless he received the blessing he wanted. Or they can recite another of the 200 times the blessing is mentioned in Scripture. The purpose of this time is to demonstrate how God's blessing changes things. It changed a 24-hour period into a Sabbath. It changed a little boy's lunch into a huge meal. And it still changes people and things today.

Then we begin with a time of affirmation when several in the congregation will stand and tell the candidate how they see God at work in his or her life. We are energized when people who know us remind us that they see evidence that God is at work within us. The devil loves to remind us of the negatives. Research shows that the human mind remembers negative things that happen to us or wrong decisions we make 14 times longer than the good things. That's no doubt why the Apostle Paul urges us to speak only those things that build up others. (Eph. 4:29) Affirming how we see God at work in someone's life is one way we can do that.

Occasionally we will sense a reluctance by some to speak to another person about the Christian characteristics that are seen in them. Some may feel that this kind of exercise is like

paying someone a cheap compliment and might somehow lead to spiritual pride. But our example in this part of the service is Jesus Himself.

When Nathanael was first introduced to Jesus (John 1:47, 48), the first words Jesus spoke of him were strong words of affirmation—and He spoke them in public: "Here is a true Israelite," Jesus observed, "in whom there is nothing false." Imagine hearing that pronouncement spoken over you by the sinless Son of God! Can we doubt that in the days ahead Nathanael would find those words an encouragement?

But there is another insight from this story that is instructive to us. Nathaniel's predictable response to Jesus was, "How do you know me?" Jesus replied: "I saw you under the fig tree before Philip called you." I hear Jesus saying something like this: "Nathanael, the very first time I saw you, even before we formally met, I saw in you a man of character. I respect that in you." If that is indeed the inference of Jesus' statement, then a trait I see in Jesus is that of one who goes looking for the best in others. That inspires me to do the same. Imagine what it might do in our families, our churches, our offices, our neighborhoods, if we were constantly searching for qualities we could affirm in others.

This is a good time for the leader to encourage the entire congregation to determine that they will declare a moratorium on criticism. In truth, criticism is the devil's counterfeit for intercessory prayer and a critical spirit can stifle the blessing gift God wishes to provide.

The other time Jesus demonstrates affirmation is even more amazing. It is recorded in the first ten verses of Luke 7 and it involves a Roman military officer. When this Centurion expresses faith in Jesus, "turning to the crowd" the story says, Jesus expresses strong affirmation of this man who is not even a member of the same church, when He says, "I have not found such great faith even in Israel." It is obvious that Jesus is not reluctant to express affirmation for that person who demonstrates the working of God in his life. I believe He would say to us, "Go and do likewise."

When several have spoken their words of encouragement, those who wish to are invited to come to the front where the candidates are seated. The members gather around, placing their hands on those being blessed, or on the shoulder of those who are touching them.

It is not a common practice in our tradition to lay hands of blessing on others. But it was

apparently a New Testament Church tradition (see for instance Acts 6:6 and 13:3). One afternoon several years ago we were kneeling in a circle around a group of members, praying for Holy Spirit power in their lives as they headed to new responsibilities, when my friend and mentor, Pastor Charles Bradford, stopped us. He said to me, "Sister Ruthie, we are not doing this right. We need to lay hands on these folks." I've never forgotten that incident because the laying on of hands is a Scriptural symbol of the blessing the Holy Spirit wants to gift to those whom the church is setting apart.

Several who wish to may pray in this circle at the front of the church. If the group is more than a handful we recommend a microphone be used so all—those in the circle and those still seated in the congregation—may hear. As they are returning to their seats we like to sing, unaccompanied, a song of dedication like, "Have Thine Own Way, Lord," or "There Shall Be Showers of Blessing!"

It is common for pastors or others who receive this hands-on blessing to tell us that other than their ordination or perhaps their baptism, this is the most meaningful experience they have ever had with the church.

When the members arrive back at their seats, the service is not over. Each person is invited to find a partner and then exchange affirmations and a blessing prayer with the laying on of hands. Couples often find this time especially meaningful. Make sure no one is overlooked. Three in a group is acceptable; two is better.

Before dismissal you may wish to ask for volunteers in the congregation to stand and describe their response to this very special occasion ... what it meant to them ... how they sense it has empowered them for further service ... how they are encouraged that they have received a new Holy Spirit filling for victory. These brief moments of testimony often prove to be a powerful encouragement to those who are there.*

*By the way, in the United States, October is Pastor Appreciation Month. Maybe that's a good time to begin a new tradition in your congregation.

Chapter 8

Your Story

On a cold, snowy January weekend my husband and I were traveling to New Jersey for an area-wide Prayer Conference. When we boarded the plane in Ft. Myers, Florida, the temperature was 72°; when we de-planed in Philadelphia it was 12° and snowing hard. But in spite of the weather, the family of God gathered to bask in the warmth of His presence. We sensed Him come near as we prayed and worshiped and studied together. It became a life-changing weekend for many of us.

As the retreat drew to a close I met two ladies from a congregation near the conference center who were obviously rejoicing over the time they had spent in God's presence. One of them, whom we'll call Gloria, was the mother of a teenage son and she had a story she was eager to tell me of what she had recently learned about God.

"He is trustworthy," Gloria said with assurance. "His promises are true." She began to tell me about her son and how he had nearly broken her heart. He had begun to run with a rough crowd who were involved in some very destructive behaviors. In anguish she had watched as he developed a crippling addiction to drugs. "We tried everything," she said. "We prayed, we begged, we scolded, we pleaded, we took away privileges ... till we finally just ran out of ideas." For several years the family lived with anguish and worry as the boy seemed to have no interest in having his life back.

"I finally came to the end of my rope," Gloria recalled, "and one afternoon I felt that I just could not go on watching him destroy himself. It was not only damaging because of the strong drugs he was using, but also because he was hanging out with a crowd that were venturing into increasingly perilous behaviors. She knew he was in danger—spiritually and physically—so she decided the time had come for her to make a 9-1-1 call to the throne room of the universe and enter into serious intercession with God, the only One she could go to with a burden this heavy.

Late that afternoon she slipped into her bedroom and closed the door. Kneeling by her bed she cried out to the Lord, "I cannot leave Your presence today until You rescue my boy. I'm going to be just like Jacob at the Brook Jabbok. I cannot let You go until You bless me. I give You my son. He is Your property. Only You can save Him, but You have told me that You are not willing that any should perish—and neither am I. You have promised to save my children and I am claiming that promise right now."

With an intensity born of love and desperation she took to God every promise she could find as He led her through His Word. And she took courage in the assurance that God had drawn near to listen to a mother's heart.

An hour went by, maybe two. Gloria told God, "I'm going to stay here in Your presence until You give me peace." And she did—and He did. She prayed and wept before the Lord, but she knew she was not alone. The promised Comforter was with her. She reminded God that His promises do not return to Him void, but He accomplishes what He has promised. She thanked Him for hearing, for answering. Finally a sweet peace came to her and she finished her prayer with a light heart.

The next day there was apparently no change. Nor the next. But five days later, her son walked into the kitchen where she was preparing dinner and said humbly, "Mom, I need help. I have reached the bottom and I can't go on any

longer like this." The prodigal son had returned, to his mother, and to his Father. She prayed with him as he accepted Christ anew into his heart and his life started over.

They were able to find a Christian rehabilitation facility that gave him further help and daily encouragement until he was stronger. At the time Gloria shared the story with me, she was virtually glowing as she said, "It's been 60 days and he is still clean, and getting stronger every day!" I spoke with her just today, weeks later, and he is still growing spiritually, attending church with the family, and still "clean."

"My encouragement to other mothers who are pleading for their children – don't give up; God is hearing your prayers."

And here is a part of the story I don't want you to miss. Since this dear mother told me her story I have had opportunity to share it with others all over this land. Each time I have told it I have seen how it has blessed and encouraged and motivated and cheered others. That's another way we bless each other. As we see what He has done in other places it gives us courage to whisper, "Do it again, Lord."

No wonder God urges us, "Let the redeemed of the Lord say so!" (Ps.107:2), because

it encourages us when we are reminded of His supreme ability to rescue the perishing. It also blesses our own hearts and helps us be victorious when we tell of His providences: "They (God's people) overcame him (the enemy) by the blood of the Lamb *and by the word of their testimony*." (Rev. 12:11, emphasis supplied) Tell your story, it may be just the nudge somebody needs.

Lucile Lacy is a long-time professor of music at Oakwood University with a story you need to hear. Listen:

"When I was a teenager, a high school teacher told me that I would never be a success—she even told me I would likely be a 'detriment to society.' No one had ever made such a sweeping negative evaluation of my potential, and I can tell you, I was devastated." But God had other intentions for Lucile.

George Peabody College for Teachers in Nashville had recently merged with Vanderbilt University and Lucile received a Masters degree there in Music Education. Following graduation she immediately began teaching college-level music classes and taught for several years.

She continues, "But I began to wonder if maybe God had bigger plans for me so I prayed, 'Lord, if it is Your will for me to pursue a doctoral

degree, please open the way.' "Unexpectedly, I was awarded a United Negro College Fund Teaching Grant for $10,000, renewable annually. This to me seemed a notable honor for one who had been told by a professional educator that I had no future. It also encouraged me to believe that God had a way of opening the door for me to continue my schooling.

"My goal was to take my doctoral work at Ohio State University. I applied, and from a pool of 400 applicants, I was one of the ten accepted into the program. It was obvious to me that God had His hand in shaping my future.

"It was a thrill to begin my work at OSU, but not long after arriving on campus I met a professor who told me that, as a Seventh-day Adventist, I had no chance of succeeding in the doctoral program. The graduate music curriculum was so tough and so competitive that he assured me it was impossible for me to complete it if I insisted on missing all the Friday evening and Saturday sessions. He sternly told me that I should either attend the classes as required or withdraw from the program.

"I knew about the promises of God to bless His children who are obedient," Lucile recalls, "and I left the professor's office determined

to complete the program and to honor God by keeping the Bible Sabbath.

"On a Friday afternoon at the end of one semester, this same professor gave our class an almost impossible 'take home' final exam. It was due the following Monday and would require extensive research in the library all weekend.

"Two hours before sunset on Friday afternoon I closed up my studies and prepared for the Sabbath. The thought of spending the next day at the campus library never entered my mind.

Saturday evening some of my classmates phoned to wish me success. They reported that the assignment was even harder than they thought it would be and they had spent all Friday evening and all day Saturday in the library and were far from finished.

"Sunday morning when the library opened, I hit the stacks. By Sunday evening, after ten hours of research, I had answered three of the exam's ten questions. It became clear that if I was going to finish this final I was going to need a lot of supernatural help, so I stopped and prayed for an hour. God knew my plight, but I wanted Him to know that I knew how much I needed Him right then. And He arrived, right on schedule.

"Reading, writing, reading, writing … I

have to admit I had become a bit anxious about getting the exam completed. Then, just a couple of hours before the library was to close, I felt impressed to get up from my study carrel and walk down the stacks. I need the exercise anyway, I reasoned. Praying silently as I walked, I soon felt hot tears streaming down my cheeks. The completed exam was due early the next morning and I was still less than half done.

"Despair began to sweep over me, when suddenly, in front of me, a book dropped from the shelf and fell open on the floor. When I reached down to pick it up some familiar words caught my eye. The book had opened to the very topic of the next question on the exam. In fact, as I read further I found the exact information I needed to answer the question. Quickly I picked up the book and hurried to my study carrel and gratefully completed that part of the exam.

"Sensing unmistakably the hand of God in leading me on the previous question, I began walking down the book stacks again when another book fell from the shelf, open to a page that provided help for another of the questions.

"One of the library assistants heard the sounds of the books falling from the shelves and came hurrying over to ask me if I knew who was throwing books. I just smiled through my tears, and assured her, 'Well, it wasn't me.' I picked up the other books from the floor and noted the page openings, rejoicing in the Lord as I did. Each time I got stuck on a question I hurried back to the stacks, and incredibly, each time God would drop a book at my feet—open to the very information I needed. That Sunday evening I discovered exactly what miracles look like!"

Can God do that? Do you mean can the God who opened a dry path through the Red Sea do that? Do you mean can the God who caused the sun to stand still do that? Do you mean can the God who restored a dead man to life do that? Those stories are recorded so that you and I will have our answer.

"As the library was about to close," Lucile continues," I finished. I was the only student in the class who completed the entire examination. I got an 'A.'"

Lucile—soon-to-be Lucile Lacy, Ph.D.—was understandably grateful, but not surprised. She knew what you and I know—God is both loving and powerful, and He still loves to bless His people. And when we tell our story, He uses it to bless others as well.

Let me tell you about Rita. You will resonate

with her story if you find yourself sometimes struggling, as she was, with her fears and uncertainty. She knew she loved Jesus, but she had a difficult time believing that He had accepted her. Could she trust Him enough to know that she really did have the gift of eternal life? It all seemed just a bit fragile in her mind.

Rita had been our hostess in Ft. Myers, Florida, following a worship service on a beautiful February afternoon. After a wonderful time of food and fellowship in her home the 20 or so of us from the church who had gathered there were preparing to leave; Rita called us together for a time of prayer.

Before we prayed together she paused and said, "If you have just another minute, I want to share my story with you. I think some of you might find encouragement in it." Then she told of her spiritual struggles, wanting so much to hear something from God, and needing peace. She recalled how she needed Him to take away her doubts and speak assurance to her heart.

Finally one day she had decided the issue was too important for her to guess about, so she went to a secluded place in her house and wept out her anguish. "God," she said, "I really need to know that You love me and will help me through this." She read all the promises of assurance she could find in Scripture.

As she paused in the quietness, she heard a response very different than she had expected. She didn't hear it with her ears, but in her heart. It was too real to miss. Going through her mind were the words of an old gospel song she hadn't sung or even thought about since she was a child many years before in a children's Bible class. The chorus of the song said,

> *"Hold fast till I come, sweet promise of heaven –*
> *The kingdom restored, to you shall be given.*
> *Come, enter My joy, sit down on My throne,*
> *Bright crowns are in waiting; hold fast till I come."*
>
> (F.E. Belden, 1886)

Now the tears were tears of joy as she accepted the words of the song as His personal message to her soul. "'Bright crowns are in waiting…' I will never be the same," she said.

Rita had the courage to tell her story and it blessed a whole roomful of people, many of them in ways she may never know. Like the Book says, "Let the redeemed of the Lord say so." Who does God want to bless with your story?

Your Story

You wish your story had more meaning,
So you could tell how you conquered all the pain.
But life's been gentle, even easy;
You've convinced yourself you don't have much to say.

So your story goes unspoken,
A testimony that's been silenced by your fears.
But let me tell you, the day God saved you,
He penned the wondrous story someone needs to hear.

Your story holds the power – giving hope to the weary on their way.
Your story tells them how this God of love still reaches out with arms of grace.
You've seen what God can do, now it's up to you to share His glory.
They're waiting to be free, wanting to believe … you have just what they need – Your story.
The cross of Christ, the sacrifice that cannot be denied.
It took as much to save you as the thief He hung beside.

Your story holds the power – giving hope to the weary on their way.
Your story tells them how this God of love still reaches out with arms of grace.
You've seen what God can do, now it's up to you to share His glory.
They're waiting to be free, wanting to believe ... you have just what they need – Your story.

Rodney Griffin*

*Rodney Griffin, composer of "Your Story" has been baritone and song writer for Greater Vision since 1993. Greater Vision is the most-awarded trio ever in Southern Gospel music. Rodney has written more than 400 gospel songs and has been chosen song writer of the year for Southern Gospel music each of the last fourteen years.

You may download this beauiful song written by Rodney Griffin and sung by Greater Vision free at www.livingblessed.org/bonus; user name: yourstory; password: 091634-1102.